*Dedicated to my husband
with love*

Listening
to the
Littlest

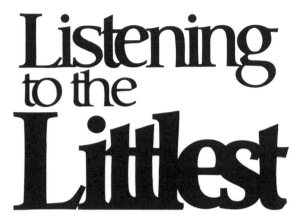

by Ruth Reardon
Illustrations by Roland Rodegast

The C.R. Gibson Company, Norwalk, Connecticut 06856

If littlest ones could know
  what only years can teach.

If littlest ones could tell
  just how they feel . . .

Maybe . . . they would talk
  like this . . .
Maybe . . . we would listen . . .

HOW DO I LEARN JUST WHO I AM?
I learn from you who I am.
Within your eyes I see
    reflected me.
Within your voice I hear
    how you see me.
You are the mirror that I look into
    and mold the image of myself.
I sense the way you hold me,
    and from your touch
        I feel my form, my shape.

And if I like what I see in
    your eyes,
        your voice,
            your touch—
My heart responds and reaches out.
Then in its reaching, grows and grows,
    until I see myself
        as separate.
That separate self—in turn—
    can love you back.
Because you taught me
    who I am,
        and I am loved.

ACCEPT ME—
    for what I am
Not what I could have been
    or even will be.
Accept me.
Acceptance must be present tense,
    with no conditions,
        and based upon reality.
If windows of your heart
    must rosy-tinted be
        you have not accepted me.
See me as I am without distortion
    of your dreams . . .
A human being, beautiful, unique.
Free to grow according to the seed
    within myself.
Accept me—
    so I need not twist myself
        to fit your pattern . . .
But resting in acceptance,
    can grow.

LET ME CRY SOMETIMES . . .
to know that I can wait,
and then, receive.
Let me cry sometimes . . .
to know I cannot always
have my way.
Let me cry sometimes . . .
to see that you are near,
but yet are separate—
to learn you do not owe me
all your time.
Let me cry sometimes . . .
to find I can amuse myself—
to learn that protests do not always
change the way things are.
Let me cry sometimes . . .
for "wait" does not mean lack of love,
but more!

WHAT ARE YOU SAYING ABOUT THE WORLD
   when you shield me too tightly?
What are you saying about me
   when you don't let me go?

Am I hearing that life is dangerous?

Am I hearing that I can't make it?

LET ME LOOK AWAY
   and see that there are others.
Let me move away
   for there are others.
Important as you are,
   and will remain,
Let me look away
   for there are others
      for us both.

HOW DO I JOIN IN, MOTHER?
How do I be a part?
I want to be accepted . . .
How do I join in, Mother?
Will they let me?
Will you help me?
Will you be a bridge
    while I need it?
Help them to understand . . .
Help me to blend . . .
How do I join in, Mother?

I NEED A "JOB."
Prepare me now in little ways
    to take responsibility
        for some things . . .
So I won't be completely shocked
    to find in later years
        that "living" means some "giving."

LETTING ME HELP
  is letting me share your world—
   letting me practice.
Dissolving ever so slowly
  walls between worlds of a child—
   and yours.
Letting me help is letting me
  feel important
   and needed.
Wanting to grow up . . .
  to be like you.

HELP ME KEEP THE SPARKLE
  in my eyes.
Feeling good about
  myself—
   lovable—
    and capable.
Then whatever limitations
  or difficulties come . . .
I can face them
  with the sparkle
   in my eyes . . .
    and in my heart.

MY FEARS ARE REAL TO ME
and telling me they're silly
won't make them disappear.
With comfort, understanding
I'll build the strength
to look at what I fear.
But now, my fears are real,
as real as yours . . .
Only the objects different.

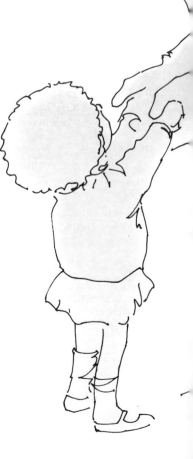

TOO LITTLE TO UNDERSTAND?
Not too little to misunderstand!
My worries grow and change to fantasies
  you'd never recognize!
Include me—(you cannot hide it anyway).
Use words, (however simple) and
  your own presence.
Including me brings reassurance
  that although "something's wrong"
    we'll be all right . . .
      together.

WHERE DID I COME FROM?
And you?
Knowing there were grandmas far, far, back
      (and grandmas I can be with now).
Knowing there are cousins, aunts, and uncles
      gives me a feeling of belonging.
Of being a part of something older,
      something wider,
            something safe.
I feel important.

CREATE A QUILT OF MEMORIES
to keep me warm.
An inner warmth that comes
from light of happy times.
Weave in the threads of holidays,
of friends and families . . .
Delights of seashore, fields,
of city parks.
The simplest happenings
traced out in love
become a pattern,
for my quilt of memories.

THERE IS NO SUBSTITUTE FOR YOU,
 your time
  and our relationship.
Giving things in place of you
 will only teach me
  to want more
   and more
    and more . . .
Because there'll be an emptiness
 more things
  can never fill.

ALWAYS MAKE TIME,
 minutes of time,
  minutes of love.
Keep showing me that you love me.
If I learn to love,
 it will be a priceless gift.
Whatever I can, or cannot, do,
 if I love,
  I'll receive so much.
So express it—giving yourself—
 hugging takes only a minute,
But the print of the hug
 on my heart
  lasts forever.

YOU LIKE TO SEE US LOOKING
so "picture-book" ideal,
but don't panic when we fight.
We need our arguments
to practice give and take
where it is safe—at home.
Stop me before I pull out all *her hair,*
but don't prolong the battle,
with your reactions.
After we have had it out,
we'll be "picture-book" ideal again,
until . . .

LET ME HAVE A "MINE"
    that no one takes,
        unless I choose to share.
And if I don't so choose,
    tell me that it's o.k.
As you respect my "mine,"
    I'll find it easier
        to let you have your "yours."

WHEN YOU'RE GOOD TO YOURSELF
you're good to me.
So, now and then, have a day away—
Buy a gift for yourself—
I'll share it, too,
for your feelings flow out to me.

WHEN YOU LEAVE, MOTHER
you don't need my permission.
It's good for you and good for me
but tell me! Don't disappear.
Better I scream my disapproval
than live in vague suspicion
that I'll find you gone again.
For then I'd have to "guard" you,
afraid to leave your side to play.
Don't disappear—tell me
that you're leaving,
and that you're coming back!
In telling me, you're also teaching me
to feel all right one day,
When I leave you . . . for short times,
and longer,
longer . . . times.

"WHERE IS JOHNNY,
Where is Johnny?
There he is, there he is—
Johnny put your hand up,
How are you?"
I sit in a circle . . .
    and listen to my name,
All eyes on me—they wait for me
    to raise my hand . . .
"Here I am."
I am here; expected and belonging—
My class, my school, my teachers, and
    my friends.
A step away from home,
    a step into the world.
A world that knows my name
    —and calls it—
"Here I am!"

HURRY, HURRY, HURRY, HURRY,
Where are we hurrying to?
Is this the way to life?
Is this the way to love?
Hurry, hurry, hurry, hurry,
    back and forth,
        forth and back.
Where are we hurrying to?
Is this the way to grow?
Is this the way to learn?
What is the hurrying for?
Missing so much—
Not stopping to touch.
Where are we hurrying to?
Will we know when we get there?
Or will we keep on
    hurrying,
        hurrying,
            hurrying . . .

SOMETIMES . . .
　　let's just blow bubbles,
For no good reason,
　　let's just blow bubbles.
Laugh a little, watch them disappear,
　　not even wonder where.
Smile and touch the rainbow colors
　　watch them float in air.
No reason why—
　　no goals—no structure.

Sometimes . . .
　　let's just
　　　　blow bubbles . . .

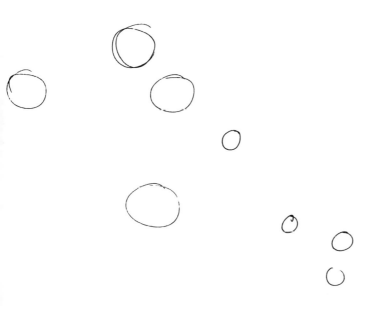

AFTER YOUR TEARS
    you saw some sun . . .
I heard your laugh—
    the dark didn't seem so black.
I heard your laugh—
    you seemed bigger and stronger.
I heard your laugh—
    I lifted my head.
I heard your laugh—
    and I laughed back.
You'll cry again,
    and you'll laugh again . . .
I'll learn tears are o.k.
    for tears aren't forever . . .

GOOD NIGHT, MOTHER,
  it's o.k.
You didn't win a prize for motherhood
  today, but it's o.k.
You haven't ruined my development
  by one bad day.
I want a human mother, not a model one.
You sure were angry at the world!
I learned a few new words
  (I won't repeat!)
Don't worry Mother—I felt your kiss.
There's always a tomorrow—
Forgiving and forgetting are easy
  when I know that I am loved!

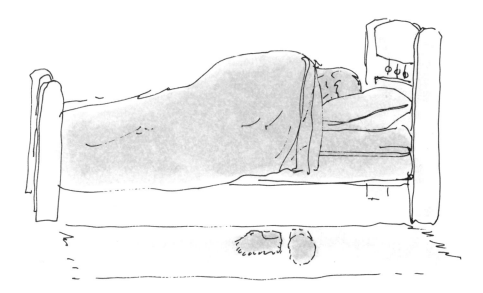

I'M NOT A TOY—
don't set me up, make me perform
for your amusement,
Or teach me words and acts to bring
a laugh.
Laugh with me, sure, but not at me.
I might decide to stay a "toy"
programmed to get attention
by my acts,
being a clown to hide my
lack of confidence in me.
Remember, I'm a person,
not a toy.

IF I HAVE SPECIAL NEEDS, REMEMBER
they are special
but I am not.
I'm not a "special child"
but a child with special needs.
Be sensitive, and make allowances.
But whenever it is possible,
treat me like all the rest.
Don't let those special needs
be all you see of me.
Give me the dignity of living
with the same rules as the others.
Not set apart,
or different,
except where I must be.
Keep me, and others,
from using handicaps!

WATCH HOW I PLAY
     if you want to know
          what I'm feeling.
Listen—
     not only to words.
I *"say it through play,"*
     so listen—
          and watch.

IF I CAN'T HIT PEOPLE . . .
     give me something that I can,
          to get my angry feelings out.
It's when I have to lock them up
     they sometimes ooze (or else explode)
          out other ways.
Disguised, but still remaining,
     causing problems.

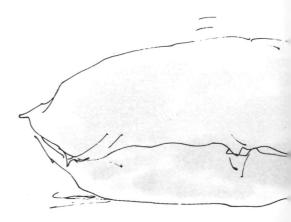

"NO" GIVES SECURITY.
When you say "no,"
    please mean it.
(Why say it, otherwise?)
I may look *pleased*
    to overrule,
But still it worries me
    to be without some limits,
        and without consistency.

TALKING TOGETHER—SHARING . . .
somehow lightens the problems.
It helps to know that other babies
like to bite and to say "no,"
to play at 3:00 a.m.
It helps to know that other mothers
sometimes wish they weren't!
It helps to listen—
to different views
to cry a little,
to laugh a lot.
Besides, I like to hear you tell
at home:
"You'll never guess what Erin's
baby did."
Makes me look like an angel!

BE YOURSELF
and only expect to be
what you are.
Parenting is not some mold
in which to pour yourself.
People just don't change to
parents.
They are always people.
Though I don't know what "parent"
means,
I like the "you"—and
you should, too!

LET ME KNOW THERE'S SOMEONE—
  always listening,
    always caring . . .
Stronger and more loving—
  than even you!

Enlarge my vision to include
  more than my eyes can see . . .
To reach out for . . . ETERNITY!
Tell me of God.

Teach me of One who listens . . .
  and listens perfectly.

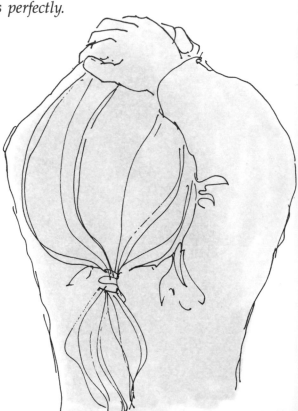

DOES HE KNOW I'M HERE?
Does He take the time to listen?
Does He care about the things I care about?
Are they important to Him . . .
And does He really love me?

So easy now for me to just believe
*   the answer's YES.*
Plant the seed of faith within my heart!
In later years, if I should struggle,
*   (with a "wiser" mind)*
That faith will still be there . . .
*   down deep . . .*
And it will blossom . . .
*   when I mature . . .*
By going back to childlike faith.

DID YOU ALWAYS TAKE IT SO FOR GRANTED—
  God's creation—
    in our own back yard?
Will you rediscover it . . .
  with me?

EACH CANDLE GIVING LIGHT
  for every year I've been here.
We're celebrating . . . ME!
I get a song, a gift, a wish—
I must be special.
You must be really glad you had ME.

DO YOU WORRY
    if you're doing right?
So much advice,
    so many books—
I grow so fast!
Are you sometimes scared?
Things balance out . . .
Too much of this, too little of that.
You try too hard, don't try enough.
Too far this way, too far the other.
Of course you'll make mistakes . . .
    but love is a great eraser!
And things will always balance out
    because
        you
           care.

ACKNOWLEDGMENTS

My deepest thanks to all who helped in so many ways:
To all the members of the staff of the Early Intervention Programs of the South Shore Mental Health Center, and the Coastal Community Counseling Center, especially Barbara Greenglass and Hilda Mahoney for their support and guidance.

To Jean and Robert Rich for their invaluable assistance.

To Charles Waitt and Nancy Hansberry.

To the many parents who have given me the privilege of teaching their children.

To my Mother, who always listened so well and my children, Dorothy, Dennis, Joanne, and Beth who are *still* teaching me to listen!

And, most of all, thanks to Linda Bristol who gave so much of herself in the creation of this book.

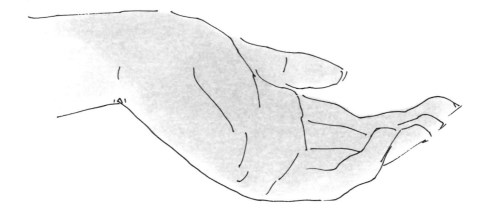

Editorial direction by Stephanie C. Oda
Designed by Roland Rodegast
Type set in Palatino Italic/Roman